from

from

poems by

JILL OSIER

PRESS

DURHAM, NORTH CAROLINA

f r o m

"This Field Wasn't Always a Field" reprinted from *Prairie Schooner*
79.3 (Fall 2005) by permission of the University of Nebraska Press.
Copyright © 2005 by the University of Nebraska Press.

Published in the United States of America

Library of Congress Cataloging-in-Publication Data

Osier, Jill
from: poems / by Jill Osier
p.   cm.
hardcover edition ISBN-13: 978-1-4951-7876-4
softcover edition ISBN-13: 978-1-4951-7875-7

Book design by Jill Osier *with* Spock and Associates

Cover art by
Larassa Kabel
Jericho, 2014
Lithograph, 30" x 22"
photo credit: Andy Lyons

Published by
BULL CITY PRESS
1217 Odyssey Drive
Durham, NC 27713

www.BullCityPress.com

CONTENTS

Small Town   3

Some Roads in Iowa   4

This Field Wasn't Always a Field   5

Edge of the World   6

Some Roads in Iowa (II)   7

From   8

Grip   9

Lake Saganaga   10

Of Unsent Letters, One   11

Kansas   12

The Horses Are Fighting   14

Mars   15

Relume   17

River   18

Ice Boat Notes   20

September   21

The Solace Is Not the Lullaby But That Anything
    Can Be a Lullaby   22

Pony   23

The Rain Falls Far   24

Brother   25

They're Saying Now That Feathers Are Mostly
    Light, That Wings Are Mostly Not There   26

Vespers   27

Requiem   28

Shell Rock Song   29

ACKNOWLEDGMENTS

Grateful acknowledgment is made to the journals where these poems originally appeared.

32 Poems: "Kansas" and "September"

Alaska Quarterly Review: "From" and "Vespers"

Beloit Poetry Journal: "Lake Saganaga" and "Pony"

Big Muddy: A Journal of the Mississippi River Valley: "Shell Rock Song" (*as* "To a Fisherman, After Years")

The Cincinnati Review: "The Rain Falls Far"

Crazyhorse: "Brother"

The Georgia Review: "They're Saying Now That Feathers Are Mostly Light, That Wings Are Mostly Not There"

The Gettysburg Review: "Mars"

Granta (granta.com): "Requiem"

Green Mountains Review: "The Horses Are Fighting"

The Iowa Review: "Edge of the World," "Some Roads in Iowa," and "Some Roads in Iowa (II)" (*as part of* "Some Roads in Iowa")

New Letters: "Of Unsent Letters, One"

Prairie Schooner: "This Field Wasn't Always a Field"

Quarterly West: "Ice Boat Notes" and "The Solace Is Not the Lullaby But That Anything Can Be a Lullaby"

The Southern Review: "Grip," "Relume," and "River"

ZYZZYVA: "Small Town"

The author wishes to thank the Poetry Society of America and Donald Revell for the honor of the Alice Fay Di Castagnola Award for a manuscript in progress.

ACKNOWLEDGMENTS

for J, J, J, J, and J

&

for D and T

SMALL TOWN

Listen. The rug is wet because
I stood here. Because
it started pouring. Because
your door was open and I was
under a tree. Because
it was raining. Because the rain
and tree both
were in your backyard. Because
so was I. Because you
weren't home. Because I knew
you were bowling. Because
I walk your road. Because your road
goes by your house. Because
I felt like a walk. Because
it was going to rain. Because your door
is never locked.

SOME ROADS IN IOWA

He lived down the street, on a dead end
known as Boulevard. A quiet boy I grew up
drawn to, he grew lean, curving hard
and away like a good pitch
or trout.

We are never loving what we think we are. Never
simply. The first thing we loved
we don't even remember: a corner
of fabric, some handle. When we loved again,
perhaps a sound, we were actually trying to hear
fabric. We listened for corners.

THIS FIELD WASN'T ALWAYS A FIELD

The paint on the hood glistens.
If she looks deep, glints of light like fish
or stars start swimming. She thinks
she's seen this before in nail polish.
She smells her fingers, checks the middle one's
last knuckle. Swollen. A crescent purpled
one side this morning. Some grounder's
bad hop she doesn't remember. The boy's still trying
to say it, leaned back on the windshield, but all the Irish
blood in the ground can't help. Quiet, quiet,
all the way home. He corners carefully
like someone older. In two years she will learn
to drive. Her temple rests in one small circle
on the window, all the blood leaving there,
a cold coming in.

EDGE OF THE WORLD

The summer my grandmother was dying my father walked me
to a carnival so my mother could sob into the living room carpet. It was
the last summer I wore red bib overalls and the red and white sailor shirt—
the summer I couldn't quite see past the logic of baseball, so after
the Babe Ruth boys took the championship, Toya Nelson and I
went looking for them. She invited herself places, which made
my mother kind of sad, but I just thought she wasn't afraid,
and what was sad about that? Her brothers had pounded this
into her, liked to string her up in a backyard tree by her feet. We
found the team at Jason Raisty's, jerseys damp, their bangs stuck
to dirty foreheads. We all sat with legs touching, watching movies
that made you squeeze your knees together, look at your hands. I
thought about hook slides. The air outside was big and quiet when we left.
I walked her home to her mother's trailer, to sleep curled next to her, her cowlick
and crooked jaw, her stubby fingers and coppery skin, her breasts always two
years behind mine.

SOME ROADS IN IOWA (II)

What toy, looking back, taught me wrong? It said
to pull apart its hemispheres, let its insides
tumble out. It said to fill the hollowness again,
matching pieces to same-shaped holes. My
many-eyed pumpkin. My few-starred sky.

I was still a girl. I watched my left foot step
into what would be a shape, saw hips
then hands follow. I left sleep for concrete
outside his basement bedroom window
and sat at the screen for the sound of his breathing.

The hollow more than shape is certain,
unfinished as some roads in Iowa
—or childhood, where the sounds started,
where we listened hard.

FROM

Sometimes the light,
as we all sat down to supper,
was, briefly, the very blue
of our collars.

We took this
in every weather
as warmth.

Later I felt us pulling
something up against the wind
of those who seemed to know
an easier way.

GRIP

The children are defending a sandbar.
The rocks they hold above their heads are large
wishes hitting the water. They do not need
to be home until dark. The trailer sits back
from a bend in the river, its front yard a puzzle
like one they found at a rummage sale once,
free since pieces were missing. Only things
like ice and snow come back. Soon the sky
will leave the river alone, won't play with it.
They've watched this happen again and again.
They've told no one.

LAKE SAGANAGA

And the whole time we fished, wishes
lined up the way shadows
refuse to. It ended up being the perfect time
for them to do this: we were all still
remembering ourselves as a family, and the light was
as it is when you trust it will hold, good enough
to know you may have had something
but lost it. Certainty always stands closest
to no thing we have.

OF UNSENT LETTERS, ONE

The man who bought the field has horses,
and they're out there now, fenced wide and loosely.
And I've been upset over the whole thing,
losing the silo pit (why have I clung to a stone
ring all these years?), but now I admit
I love to see them. I've never owned a horse.
I don't remember, fully, the last time I was on one,
but they fill, nonetheless, an emptiness.
There are several places at the edge of town
where horses are kept:
two in the pasture by the river, two more
behind the barn on Stockyard Street,
a young mare who walks the fence with me
along the gravel road, a restless one
bucking in his own circles off the old highway,
two watching as I head out toward the cemetery,
and now these—there are three—behind my house.
I find I want to watch them all the time.
It seems more important than anything else
I could be doing right now. When the sun
comes up over the hill, they are there,
perfect and restful. When I come home,
they are grazing, still oblivious. I go out
while their backs have the moon on them,
the air thick, my feet wet with alfalfa. At night
they are the darkest shadows in the field.

KANSAS

It's midnight in Kansas.
The mother goes to wake the daughter.
The ballplayer's bruises rise to the surface.
Heat has held the daughter, and trees
are bent over in the yard, not from snow.
The girl rises and bends,
tying her shoes in the kitchen's dark.
The grandmother has tied bricks to the ends
of the branches.
No one is on the road.
The fields sweat into the air, a mild stew.
The ballplayer rolls over. His sheets are wet.
Mother and daughter come from the garage
leading bony bikes.
The grandmother goes to the quilt.
The girl's arms reach for handlebars.
Pedaling hard, she can imagine wind.
There are stars. This is as dark
intended. This is as light
as she will be.
The ballplayer snores softly, one hand
badly scuffed.
The quilt, unfinished, is already
heavier than the air.
She pedals faster, and the trees look
like they never do drawn, wind
more and more like her mother's voice,

almost there, almost gone.
Hung on the wall, the quilt would sag
like a carcass being drained.
It could smother a body like a body.

THE HORSES ARE FIGHTING

They stand scattered and not
facing each other. Like black-eyed
Susans lining the highway, or sisters
angry in some small kitchen.

The goats, they traipse a diagonal
through knee-high meadow,
following head to tail. Then
one decides to feed. Suddenly
they are strangers.

But how elegant animals seem
these weeks after your funeral, each
quiet despite a whole field, content
with any fresh mouthful.

MARS

It's as if I sit on my overturned bucket
in the middle of the grass and watch,
from a distance, a garden rot.

For years it did not haunt me like this,
the image of my siblings in the rows, my sister
all brown in a tube top, my little brother sometimes
just missing. It would get hotter, my mother
insisted, so, morning sun on us, we picked.

Something happened today,
an honesty I may have missed
except I was swimming
in a small-town river. This river,
like any other, has had its chances,
has taken all of them. Today
I thought I saw it reconsider.

A clear, sunlit day is hard
in the way it is full with itself,
not waiting for you.
The river, it turns out,
is not waiting.

It was sunny the day
my mother left, taking my brother
in the heavy black-and-white

checkered stroller. There was sun
at the curb where I finally stopped
and studied close the makeup
of concrete.

Tonight bodies will shine
with old light. Some will never
be this close again.

RELUME

It is not morning but the very other side of morning
when the birthday boy tries to rake from the river
balloons he'd thrown in brick-tied,
angry at his sister. Their color now at dusk,
as they float like a family of pink soup bowls upturned, blooms
hard in his chest.

RIVER

The river is a river again,
its grayish shelves saving
a green stain deep inside.

One large piece of ice the size
of a baby blanket spins,
caught. You can bet
it will break. Or watch it
all day, softening.

Every river gives up
something, even if it's shells
for a small, brick factory
making buttons on its bank.

The river is a river again, so try. Trying
is sometimes rewarded. Guess when
the ice will crack. Guess the weight
of this wheel. Guess how many
steps it would take holding one arm
of a dead branch.

The year's first rain will be taken
like collection, confession,
the river spilling over
what it cannot take.

The river is a river again, and all
it ever was is there still: the local
genius's latest scam, the bones of carp
and bluegill, the secrets behind that
woman's skull, busted.

ICE BOAT NOTES

The seasons are always beating us
to the best ideas. This one's spectrum
siphons to bare, to a naked release
of birds. I know. I followed them
like clues, all the way to where the ground
gets shy, dipping down to little creeks, and a huge gray
tank was already there, rusting in the forest like a submarine.

SEPTEMBER

The farmers got the call on their CBs and came from all over town, their semis lined up on the gravel like toys. They blowtorched holes at the bottom of the bin and had some vacuum thing to suck the grain out faster. Still, it would take a while, which is why the family sat out in lawn chairs, watching the firemen. Margaret too. She could not be convinced to wait in the house. Her husband George was somewhere in the corn, working his way down to the auger when his son-in-law turned it off. He would be dark, the firemen knew, when they pulled him out, and they tried to stand tight, shoulder to shoulder, but Margaret, she pushed and broke through like a newborn.

THE SOLACE IS NOT THE LULLABY
BUT THAT ANYTHING CAN BE A LULLABY

When the German shopkeeper died, they said, *Go back*
to what you know. So there was math. There was standing
at the stove stirring soup until my father came home.
There were bruised train cars and an untruth,
day and night, shadowing the town's streets.
When authorities found it curled asleep
outside his house, their questions
fell into the dark grass. There was a beating
of silence then, until it was a new quiet
they had to pick up and carry away.

PONY

The day my mother was bowled over by the neighbor's black and white miniature
staked in the field was a day of clarity and a tidy loop like that of an owl,
or an ice rink, or hair being braided.

I found her in a quiet violet-gray at one end of the couch.
No light was on her.

The years I spent in the mountains left me unable to recover her face. A sliver
I could grasp at a time, phases of it like a moon's, but never the thing whole.

There is something we take from the violet hour because we need it.
And everything we take resembles what we took before.

I thought it was her father's death that held her those hours normally kept
for us, our supper, our pain. She said she'd tried to hug its neck, to bury
her face in the mane.

THE RAIN FALLS FAR

That Easter we painted porcelain rabbits and chicks. We were
too young to know what chicks couldn't be, and our mother
never said different. She let us paint them blue. She let us slide
around on the red linoleum and eat chocolate chip cookie cereal.
When you take your family and live in someone else's basement,
you take yourself to a new level. Your children playing on a fake
black leather couch seem to fall against it like snow. They look
to you like snow falling in the house, and it's true—you create
a new season, the pool table kept like a corpse, rooms closet-cold.
Your youngest two at night sneak up the stairs to find the sculpture
sometimes lit: a young boy and girl strolling beneath an umbrella.
Your children share the top stair, which is soil-level and also their sky.

BROTHER

This was long after the sun, and time
was a band that played as a great swath of light that ran
ringing the horizon and drew us to it.

We were a different kind of fool then, trimmed
stiff by patterns like stars we might forget
except they held the night and sidewalks through it. And you

with your frog heart beating. This was before I saw boats
as cradles, or bad, before any man
had said they were a graveyard. Now I see us

just before we started to change our course, simple crafts
our ships, our sails
such blankets hung from our arms.

THEY'RE SAYING NOW THAT FEATHERS ARE MOSTLY LIGHT, THAT WINGS ARE MOSTLY NOT THERE

But sometimes it's warm enough for the neighbor
to stand in the field

and brush out her horse's tail. She knows the sun
slips through it.

The horse, two-toned, is losing a winter coat, the day
a world

slipping through its own hands. Dusk will lead them
out to a road

that leads out of town, and she'll teach it how to walk this way,
through shadow.

VESPERS

Tonight my neighbor's burning
a fire next to his trailer.

I catch glimpses of his red cap
through the smoke.

The people I've watched die
said, finally, *You smell good*

or *Your hands are cold* or *You've left me
more confused than ever.*

Outside the yard goes black.
My neighbor's wife goes to him

by flashlight, and he bends
to greet the dogs.

REQUIEM

Across the street, two boys begin to bury
a girl in leaves. Kneeling at her side
they show her how to cover her face—*don't
forget to breathe*, I imagine they tell her,
when what they really should say is, *Try
to remember the smell of sun through it all. It's
a rare courtship.* I watch her help,
gathering the leaves to her like love,
hiding herself. No matter how many, it's
the same heavy. One leaf will find its way
beneath her shirt, another will tickle her lip.
What she'll hear is almost like breathing,
and it must be the leaves. Sounds beyond love,
sounds beyond love... Remember, I would tell her,
there are such things.

SHELL ROCK SONG

It's less important why
and more important where
we leave some things.

I should have learned
this by now, grown
in a small river town,

collecting, as a girl,
colored stones from clear,
shallow depths. Before

home, they'd have dried
themselves dull. They left
my pockets wet.

Today at the river
only the geese were there,
held in glare of winter sun.

Again I tried to take
the shape of solitude
at the side of a river.

Again I stood motionless,
yet they were more still.
I stayed, adoring them,

over an hour in the cold,
waiting, I think,
for them to love me.

Then I walked home.

JILL OSIER is the author of *from* (Bull City Press),
winner of the 2017 Alice Fay Di Castagnola Award,
and *Should Our Undoing Come Down Upon Us White* (Bull
City Press), winner of the 2013 Frost Place Chapbook
Competition, as well as a letterpress chapbook, *Bedful of
Nebraskas* (sunnyoutside).